Landscape Architect Registration Examination

# LARE Review Section 1 Sample Exam

*Project and Construction Administration*

Second Edition

Matt Mathes, PLA

**LARE REVIEW, SECTION 1 SAMPLE EXAM: PROJECT AND CONSTRUCTION ADMINISTRATION Second Edition**

© 2009 Professional Publications, Inc. All rights reserved.
© 2019 Matt Mathes, PLA. All rights reserved.
March 2018 -Author acquisition of book rights.

All content is copyrighted by Matt Mathes, PLA. No part, either text or image, may be used for any purpose other than personal use. Reproduction, modification, storage in a retrieval system or retransmission, in any form or by any means, electronic, mechanical, or otherwise, for reasons other than personal use, without prior written permission from the publisher is strictly prohibited. For written permission, contact author at: msmathes@gmail.com

Printed in the United States of America.

Matt Mathes, PLA
Richland, WA
msmathes@gmail.com

ISBN: 978-1-944887-40-7
eISBN: 978-1-944887-39-1

Library of Congress Control Number: 2008935476

# Table of Contents

Preface and Acknowledgments ................................................................................. v

Introduction .............................................................................................................. vii

How to Use This Book ............................................................................................. xi

**Problems**
- Communication ............................................................................................. 3
- Standards of Practice .................................................................................... 6
- Contract Administration ............................................................................. 10
- Construction Evaluation ............................................................................. 13
- Construction Practices ................................................................................ 15

**Solutions**
- Communication ........................................................................................... 21
- Standards of Practice .................................................................................. 24
- Contract Administration ............................................................................. 28
- Construction Evaluation ............................................................................. 31
- Construction Practices ................................................................................ 34

# Preface and Acknowledgments

A successful landscape architect must be able to understand contracts and project member responsibilities, coordinate the construction process and team, and assess the design and construction project phases. The Landscape Architect Registration Exam (LARE) tests applicants on these skills, and this book, *LARE Review, Section 1 Sample Exam: Project and Construction Administration,* was written to help you assess your readiness for these problems on the exam.

**This book is for LARE Section 1 preparation** with some crossover to Section 4 exam content. Different from the first edition, this book's second edition reflects the most current CLARB specifications for the LARE. Problems and Solutions have been reorganized into the topic categories for this exam area: communication, standards of practice, contract administration, construction evaluation, and construction practices. New problems have been written and a few problems have been revised to reflect the exam's format established in 2017.

Many of the problems in this book make use of my colleagues' professional experiences. These acknowledgments highlight those professionals who most shaped my ideas for problems.

For problem ideas on landscape architecture practice regulations, my appreciation goes to attorneys Steve Goldblatt of the University of Washington, Robert L. Guyer, and Alex Schatz, as well as staff during 2004 to 2006 at ASLA Government Affairs in Washington, D.C.

For problem ideas about environmental zoning and growth management, recognition goes to my attorney Jay A. Goldstein; plus several quasi-judicial hearing examiners who conducted numerous local land-use hearings that I staffed and appeared in as an expert witness between 1999 and 2005 in the greater Seattle region. These land use and permit appeal hearings provided problem ideas for subdivisions, permits, regulations for trees, water quality, wetlands and streams, code enforcements, ethics, and appeals.

For finance, commercial lending, and engineering problem ideas, my thanks go to Mark McCloud Griggs, owner and founder of a successful engineering company and an international company.

For previewing some content in this book, my thanks go to students and faculty in the professional practice course at Louisiana State University Robert S. Reich School of Landscape Architecture.

Much appreciation goes to PPI's very capable technical staff team in 2007 for the original edition title *LARE Review, Section A Sample Exam: Project and Construction Administration*. The cover was prepared by Sam Hawkins, Benchmark Design Studio and Marcia Breece.

Finally, my deepest appreciation goes to my wife Kathy who encouraged me to write this practice exam book and its second edition.

Matt Mathes, PLA
Author & Publisher

# Introduction

### About the LARE

Successful completion of the Landscape Architect Registration Examination (LARE) is the minimum standard exam required for licensure as a landscape architect in the United States, U.S. territories, and Canada. The LARE is administered by the Council of Landscape Architectural Registration Boards (CLARB). Once licensed in any state, you can establish a record with CLARB, which can expedite the reciprocity process when applying for licensure in other states or provinces.

The LARE consists of four sections. CLARB website gives information about the exam and the availability of reference materials covering all LARE sections, and has links to CLARB resources.

CLARB provides detailed specifications for each exam section on its website. Since the test varies each time it is administered, the number of problems in each subject can shift slightly. But reviewing the exam specifications gives an overview of the subject matter covered and can guide your preparation.

### What to Bring to the Exam

For the multiple-choice sections, you should bring two forms of ID—one of which should be a photo ID—with you to the exam site.

You are not permitted to bring any reference materials, calculators, pencils, pens, paper, or food into the testing room. You will be provided with a calculator, a whiteboard, and an erasable marker when you check in. Personal items must be left in a locker that will be provided. Cell phones, pagers, devices with a computer memory chip, and devices with alphanumerical keyboards are not permitted at the test site.

# LARE Review, Section 1 Sample Exam

## Successful Exam Preparation

The first step in preparing for the LARE is to confirm the application deadlines and prerequisites for submitting an application. Most states have an application submission deadline three to four months prior to the exam date, so you should be sure to meet all experience requirements prior to the application due date (not just the exam date). Although not all states require professional experience to sit for the exam, the confidence and skill set needed to pass come from having a few years of professional experience in a diverse landscape architecture practice.

You should conduct many study sessions in preparation for the exam. Problem-solving speed and confidence come from practice. It is always in your best interest to observe good work habits and exercise sound time management during study sessions. You should become accustomed to minor distractions during study sessions; the testing centers often provide their own share of distractions and discomforts.

The *Exam Specifications* can be downloaded from the CLARB website, is a critical exam-preparation tool. The exam specifications and other indispensable information on exam content. You should be familiar with all four sections of the *LARE*.

Your local chapter of the American Society of Landscape Architects (ASLA) may offer exam preparatory sessions, which present good opportunities for gaining first-hand insight into the exam and for meeting other candidates who might be interested in forming study groups.

## Problem-Solving Strategies

The LARE problems change from year to year. However, the nature and format of the problems will be similar across all exams, and getting familiar with the problem types is an effective way to prepare.

Most multiple-choice problems present four options, one of which is correct; however, multiple-response problems may have up to nine options, and more than one will be correct. In a multiple-response problem, you are told how many of the options are correct, and you must select all the correct options and none of the incorrect ones to receive credit for a correct answer. Multiple-response problems are worth one point for a correct answer, the same as for all problems.

Multiple-choice sections may contain quantitative or nonquantitative problems. Nonquantitative problems fall into two general categories: (1) "basic recall" problems, which require you to name, identify, or remember the correct term or concept from a list, and (2) "complex" or "situational" problems, which require you to apply a principle, concept, or skill, make a judgment, or otherwise address a complex situation as a competent landscape architect.

To solve nonquantitative problems, you should start by reading the problem statement only, and should then formulate an answer before looking at any of the given options. This approach promotes better recall and helps avoid confusion caused by seeing similar terms presented in the options. Once you determine the correct answer, read the options and select the corresponding answer choice (or choices, in the case of a multiple-response problem).

Incorrect answers on the LARE do not count against the total score, so it is in your best interest to answer every problem. A good, time-conserving approach is to work through the entire exam quickly, answering all problems that can be confidently addressed, and flagging the ones that will require more thoughtful analysis. In the remaining time, go over the unaddressed problems in a second pass, working through the more complex solutions. If any problems are still unanswered near the end of the exam time limit, eliminate any options you know to be incorrect and then make a reasonable guess among the remaining ones.

## Additional Reference Materials

For construction and contract administration, I recommend the following resources.

- Abbett, Robert C. *Engineering Contracts and Specifications*. John Wiley & Sons.
- Clough, Richard H. and Glenn A. Sears. *Construction Contracting*. John Wiley & Sons.
- Hardie, Glenn M. *Construction Contracts and Specifications*. Reston Publishing Company.
- Hinze, Jimmie. *Construction Contracts*. McGraw-Hill.
- Poage, Waller S. *Plans, Specs and Contracts for Building Professionals*. R.S. Means.

I also recommend the *Handbook of Professional Practice*, by Lane Marshall, FASLA, which is an early version of his book, *Guidelines to Professional Practice*, for information about project administration; plus the *Regulation of the Profession*, by Alex Schatz, ASLA, for topics pertaining to health, safety, and welfare, liability, construction related claims, and professional regulation by states.

# How To Use This Book

### Using This Book as a Student or Professional

This book is organized according to the LARE exam subjects pertaining to project and construction administration. To optimize the benefits of this book, you should first work through all the problems, selecting the most likely answer from among the options presented. When finished, you can score your exam and analyze the results by checking the solutions in the back of the book, comparing the given solutions against your own problem-solving approaches, and assessing whether your approaches follow the same logic and reach the same conclusions. Based on this analysis, you can identify areas for improvement and tailor the next phase of study to address those knowledge gaps. Refer to the list of additional references on page 9 to supplement your study.

### Using This Book as an Instructor

Though lecture can be an indispensible tool when preparing for the LARE, students and professionals benefit most from solving problems. The *LARE Review, Section 1 Sample Exam* was designed to be used in a variety of classroom settings (such as accredited programs, exam prep classes and workshops, etc.). It may be used in its entirety to mimic the actual exam, or problems can be assigned in exam subcategories. Because working through solutions and explaining how to solve problems is an invaluable process, lectures should include reviewing all problems and solutions—especially those of difficulty.

The *LARE Review, Section 1 Sample Exam* may be used at the beginning of a course or workshop to assess strengths and weaknesses, or at the end to allow students or professionals to practice the skills and techniques they have learned, and to check their understanding of the material. The list of additional reference materials on page 9 may also be used for additional exam study or assigned reading.

# Problems

1. Ⓐ Ⓑ Ⓒ Ⓓ
2. Ⓐ Ⓑ Ⓒ Ⓓ
3. Ⓐ Ⓑ Ⓒ Ⓓ
4. Ⓐ Ⓑ Ⓒ Ⓓ
5. Ⓐ Ⓑ Ⓒ Ⓓ
6. Ⓐ Ⓑ Ⓒ Ⓓ
7. Ⓐ Ⓑ Ⓒ Ⓓ
8. Ⓐ Ⓑ Ⓒ Ⓓ
9. Ⓐ Ⓑ Ⓒ Ⓓ
10. Ⓐ Ⓑ Ⓒ Ⓓ
11. Ⓐ Ⓑ Ⓒ Ⓓ
12. Ⓐ Ⓑ Ⓒ Ⓓ
13. Ⓐ Ⓑ Ⓒ Ⓓ
14. Ⓐ Ⓑ Ⓒ Ⓓ
15. Ⓐ Ⓑ Ⓒ Ⓓ
16. Ⓐ Ⓑ Ⓒ Ⓓ
17. Ⓐ Ⓑ Ⓒ Ⓓ
18. Ⓐ Ⓑ Ⓒ Ⓓ
19. Ⓐ Ⓑ Ⓒ Ⓓ
20. Ⓐ Ⓑ Ⓒ Ⓓ
21. Ⓐ Ⓑ Ⓒ Ⓓ
22. Ⓐ Ⓑ Ⓒ Ⓓ
23. Ⓐ Ⓑ Ⓒ Ⓓ
24. Ⓐ Ⓑ Ⓒ Ⓓ
25. Ⓐ Ⓑ Ⓒ Ⓓ
26. Ⓐ Ⓑ Ⓒ Ⓓ
27. Ⓐ Ⓑ Ⓒ Ⓓ
28. Ⓐ Ⓑ Ⓒ Ⓓ
29. Ⓐ Ⓑ Ⓒ Ⓓ
30. Ⓐ Ⓑ Ⓒ Ⓓ
31. Ⓐ Ⓑ Ⓒ Ⓓ
32. Ⓐ Ⓑ Ⓒ Ⓓ
33. Ⓐ Ⓑ Ⓒ Ⓓ
34. Ⓐ Ⓑ Ⓒ Ⓓ
35. Ⓐ Ⓑ Ⓒ Ⓓ
36. Ⓐ Ⓑ Ⓒ Ⓓ
37. Ⓐ Ⓑ Ⓒ Ⓓ
38. Ⓐ Ⓑ Ⓒ Ⓓ
39. Ⓐ Ⓑ Ⓒ Ⓓ
40. Ⓐ Ⓑ Ⓒ Ⓓ
41. Ⓐ Ⓑ Ⓒ Ⓓ
42. Ⓐ Ⓑ Ⓒ Ⓓ
43. Ⓐ Ⓑ Ⓒ Ⓓ
44. Ⓐ Ⓑ Ⓒ Ⓓ
45. Ⓐ Ⓑ Ⓒ Ⓓ
46. Ⓐ Ⓑ Ⓒ Ⓓ
47. Ⓐ Ⓑ Ⓒ Ⓓ
48. Ⓐ Ⓑ Ⓒ Ⓓ
49. Ⓐ Ⓑ Ⓒ Ⓓ
50. Ⓐ Ⓑ Ⓒ Ⓓ
51. Ⓐ Ⓑ Ⓒ Ⓓ
52. Ⓐ Ⓑ Ⓒ Ⓓ
53. Ⓐ Ⓑ Ⓒ Ⓓ
54. Ⓐ Ⓑ Ⓒ Ⓓ
55. Ⓐ Ⓑ Ⓒ Ⓓ
56. Ⓐ Ⓑ Ⓒ Ⓓ
57. Ⓐ Ⓑ Ⓒ Ⓓ
58. Ⓐ Ⓑ Ⓒ Ⓓ
59. Ⓐ Ⓑ Ⓒ Ⓓ
60. Ⓐ Ⓑ Ⓒ Ⓓ
61. Ⓐ Ⓑ Ⓒ Ⓓ
62. Ⓐ Ⓑ Ⓒ Ⓓ
63. Ⓐ Ⓑ Ⓒ Ⓓ
64. Ⓐ Ⓑ Ⓒ Ⓓ
65. Ⓐ Ⓑ Ⓒ Ⓓ
66. Ⓐ Ⓑ Ⓒ Ⓓ
67. Ⓐ Ⓑ Ⓒ Ⓓ
68. Ⓐ Ⓑ Ⓒ Ⓓ
69. Ⓐ Ⓑ Ⓒ Ⓓ
70. Ⓐ Ⓑ Ⓒ Ⓓ

# Communication

**1.** Consensus decision making does NOT

    (A) use a group facilitator

    (B) discard minority held opinions

    (C) limit the number of applicable participants

    (D) allow for proposal modifications

**2.** A town is redesigning the downtown streetscape with the objective of increasing merchant revenues. To quickly reach a design consensus between public officials, merchants, and residents, the town implements a charrette. A charrette is a

    (A) multi-day, problem-orientated process

    (B) detailed plan authored by a select few

    (C) low-cost brainstorming session

    (D) one-day community workshop

**3.** Which of the following actions could a planning commission implement in order to reach consensus on a long range, regional planning proposal?

    I. interview key community informants and stakeholders

    II. distribute a mail-out/mail-in questionnaire to a random sample of community residents

    III. administer a telephone survey to a statistically significant, random sample of community residents

    IV. provide a link to a web-based questionnaire and/or survey on the community's internet homepage

    (A) I and II

    (B) III and IV

    (C) I, II, and III

    (D) I, II, III, and IV

**4.** The purpose of taking minutes during a project meeting is to

    (A) record meeting proceedings

    (B) note which tasks are assigned to whom

    (C) act as the official record of the meeting

    (D) all of the above

**5.** For a private property improvement project, the landscape contractor is responsible for
   I. looking at site access
   II. all site construction work as identified by the Construction Documents
   III. estimating a bid price based on physical analysis of the site and related technical reports
   III. determining the appropriate construction strategy by assessing site access, magnitude of work and materials needed, and time available
   IV. submitting mechanics lien affidavits before final payment may be made
   (A) I
   (B) I and II
   (C) II, III, and IV
   (D) I, II, III, IV, and V

**6.** A landscape architect and a subconsulting civil engineer designed a project's runoff water to be collected and conveyed to an onsite stormwater facility. After completion, a storm caused a release of water that was less than the minimum design-storm event volume that was required to be retained onsite. The runoff flooded a downstream property. Which of the following are possible consequences of the runoff damage?
   I. tort liability for trespass
   II. property damage claim paid by the contractor
   III. local code violation for unlawful water discharge
   IV. breach of contract or negligence claim from property owner to landscape architect
   (A) I and II
   (B) I, II, and III
   (C) II, III, and IV
   (D) I, II, III, and IV

**7.** Registered professionals on a county's staff designed a stream bypass pipe to relieve water flow when it is larger than the stream's available channels and culverts. Though the staff performed analysis reports before the pipe was installed, siltation and sediment accumulated along the frontage of several properties. Property damage claims were then filed against the county. The county is
   I. not liable because registered staff designed the pipe
   II. liable because the county's design and project caused the damage
   III. liable even if the county is insured by professional liability insurance coverage
   IV. would have been protected if a private consultant with professional liability coverage had designed the project
   (A) I and II
   (B) I, II, and III
   (C) II, III, and IV
   (D) I, II, III, and IV

# Problems

**8.** A landscape architect is assessing a project's utility plan. A utility plan usually includes

   (A) stormwater drainage

   (B) sanitary sewer and septic systems

   (C) paved areas, terraces, and walls

   (D) both A and B

**9.** A landscape architect is the primary consultant for a park design project that is in the beginning stages of design. The client has asked the landscape architect to demonstrate how services will be coordinated with other project consultants and design team members. To meet the client's request, the landscape architect should set up which type of meeting?

   (A) teleconference using voice-over internet protocol

   (B) post-construction conference involving all consultants and design team members

   (C) pre-submittal conference with all consultants and design team members to discuss the client's competitive criteria

   (D) project kickoff to discuss client needs followed by sending out minutes

**10.** A firm is looking to add new members to its landscape architecture workgroup. Which of the following methods would best ensure a balanced workgroup is created?

   (A) administer personality tests to all candidates

   (B) administer a commercially available management and leadership style assessment to all candidates

   (C) have select members of the existing workgroup conduct their own interviews of candidates, then compare notes prior to hiring

   (D) conduct regular workgroup meetings

**11.** The north side of a streetscape has larger trees than the south side. The main street runs east to west and has two-story buildings on both sides, with 10 ft setbacks from building faces to property limits. As part of a downtown redevelopment plan, the city has hired a landscape architect to help retain south-side businesses that are contemplating relocation. The landscape architect's first step in organizing the project team should be to

   (A) conduct a site analysis to find out why trees are larger on the north side of street

   (B) recruit an economist to perform a market study of businesses, customers, and competitive factors facing existing businesses

   (C) advise the city that design measures cannot be used to retain businesses who want to leave

   (D) allow the project architect to decide the first step

12. Two weeks into a project scheduled to last one year, project members are engaged in a standstill conflict, as each is fighting to implement their own ideas. This stage of small-group dynamics is called

    (A) performing
    (B) norming
    (C) forming
    (D) storming

13. Who are the parties involved in an agreement for professional services?

    (A) tenant and property owner
    (B) contractor and subcontractor
    (C) consultant and owner
    (D) owner and contractor

14. A landscape architect is the lead consultant for a park design project in the middle stages of design. A meeting has been scheduled to check in with the project's consultants and design team members, and an agenda is required. Which of the following is NOT true regarding the meeting's agenda?

    (A) specifies the meeting date, time, and location
    (B) is not distributed until the day of the meeting
    (C) is task orientated
    (D) prioritizes items of discussion

## Standards of Practice

15. Which of the following is a breach of ethics?

    (A) disclosing financial interests in a private project
    (B) respecting confidence requested by a private sector client where information, if disclosed, could be damaging to the client
    (C) inflating the cost estimate of bid documents when the firm's fee is based on a percentage of estimated construction costs
    (D) maintaining a social relationship with a private client while under contract for services to the client

16. A project is behind schedule and the client has asked the landscape architect for a revised timeline. To estimate the project's shortest completion time by analyzing only essential, interconnected activities, the landscape architect would apply principles from which of the following?

    (A) value engineering
    (B) work breakdown structure
    (C) project management plan
    (D) critical path method

**17.** A registered landscape architect has reason to believe that another registered landscape architect has violated the professional codes of ethics. The landscape architect should
   I. report the information to the appropriate committee
   II. confront the other landscape architect directly
   III. do nothing
   IV. seek legal counsel
   (A) I
   (B) III
   (C) I and IV
   (D) II and IV

**18.** According to the Council of Landscape Architectural Registration Board (CLARB) *Rules of Professional Conduct*, a licensed landscape architect may NOT
   (A) sign or seal drawings, specifications, reports, or other professional work without direct professional knowledge or supervisory control
   (B) offer gifts of nominal value to an existing or prospective client
   (C) disclose being compensated for making public statements
   (D) be the judge of contract performance

**19.** In confidence, a client informs the landscape architect that a site wetland area was filled despite the architect's previous advice to protect the wetland area. The landscape architect should
   I. report the incident to the appropriate jurisdiction
   II. terminate services with the client
   III. not breach the client's confidentiality
   (A) I
   (B) III
   (C) I and II
   (D) II and III

**20.** To negotiate and prepare client/landscape architect precontract agreements, a landscape architect should
   I. elicit the client's intentions and needs
   II. identify relevant laws, rules, and regulations
   III. coordinate and conduct field investigations
   IV. prepare site inventories
   V. formulate project guidelines
   (A) II and V
   (B) II, III, and IV
   (C) I, III, IV, and V
   (D) I, II, III, IV, and V

21. A federal agency is looking for a consulting firm to work on a federal project that will cost approximately $100,000. To notify firms of this job opportunity, the agency would most likely use which of the following?
    (A) a Commerce Business Daily (CBD) advertisement
    (B) *Federal Jobs Digest*
    (C) an advertisement in the *Federal Register*
    (D) a Federal Business Opportunities (FBO) listing

22. A city's specifications and requirements for fence height, minimum lot widths, and minimum lot size would be found in the regulations titled
    I. Development Criteria
    II. Zoning Standards
    III. Contracting Requirements
    IV. City Charter
    V. Resolutions
    (A) I
    (B) I and II
    (C) II and V
    (D) III and IV

23. For a multi-year, multi-million dollar project, tracking schedule and cash flow performance would most likely require
    (A) project management software
    (B) a wall chart
    (C) a Gantt chart
    (D) a list of milestone dates

24. A landscape architect at an established, private consulting firm is starting a new project. Which of the following should the landscape architect do first?
    (A) assign a project number and create contract and correspondence file folders
    (B) coordinate with consultants or design team members
    (C) prepare statements of estimated construction costs
    (D) review shop drawings

25. The person most likely to prepare a daily log of Requests for Information, Architect's Supplemental Instructions, payment requests, shop drawings, and change orders would be the
    (A) construction administration coordinator
    (B) project manager
    (C) clerk of works
    (D) jobsite superintendent

# Problems

**26.** Which of the following schedule delays could a landscape architect be held responsible for?

- (A) periodic site visits and/or reviews of specified technical submittals for the irrigation system
- (B) site inspections and submittals of products conducted by the owner
- (C) safety regulations that temporarily stop the project until complied with
- (D) labor negotiations

**27.** A landscape architect is serving as the program manager of a large, master planned community, and is overseeing several other design firms that are designing public outdoor areas. During the construction phase, a faulty product that could result in injury or death was brought to the attention of the landscape architect. If the landscape architect does not take action and a fatality to a third party using the site results from the product failure, the landscape architect could face

  I. tort liability for gross negligence
  II. wrongful death claim
  III. local code violation
  IV. breach of contract claim from the property owner

- (A) I and II
- (B) I, II, and III
- (C) I, II, and IV
- (D) I, II, III, and IV

**28.** Layout plans for a shade structure in a public park were prepared correctly by the landscape architect; however, the surveyor erroneously staked the proposed foundation's elevation. The discovery of the staking error occurred after concrete forms were already in place, requiring the surveyor to bring a field crew out a second time and the contractor to reset the forms. The contractor would use which of the following to adjust the total cost to fix the foundation?

- (A) overdraft
- (B) backdraft
- (C) backcharge
- (D) overcharge

**29.** A bid price encompasses a landscape contractor's cost summary for

  I. site preparation
  II. site clearing
  III. furnishing and installing all specified materials
  IV. providing necessary equipment and labor crews to complete the work on time
  V. operation overhead expenses and profit

- (A) II and V
- (B) III, IV, and V
- (C) I, II, IV, and V
- (D) I, II, III, IV, and V

**30.** A project site's existing conditions would be listed in the Construction Specification Institute's 2004 MasterFormat™ division

(A) 00
(B) 01
(C) 02
(D) 03

## Contract Administration

**31.** After a contract has been signed, the work, contract time limit, or contract amount (or sum) may be changed through which of the following?
  I. Construction Change Directive, AIA form G714™
  II. Architect's Supplemental Instruction, AIA form G710™
  III. Change Order, AIA form G701™
  IV. General Conditions of the Contract for Construction, AIA form A201™

(A) I
(B) I and III
(C) II and IV
(D) II, III, and IV

**32.** Bid addenda are NOT appropriate to use

(A) when a Request for Information (RFI) is submitted
(B) to change a bid date
(C) to revise the bid documents
(D) after a contract is awarded

**33.** The owner of a downtown condominium project has asked the contractor to sign a nondisclosure agreement as part of the contract. The contract also stipulates "time is of the essence." Which of the following constitutes a breach of contract by the contractor?

(A) releasing project financials to the city, banks, or real estate agents
(B) disclosing information that could be damaging to the owner
(C) failing to complete the project within the allowed timeframe
(D) all of the above

**34.** A third party is injured on a construction jobsite. Which of the following will cover the third party's personal injury claim?

(A) general liability insurance
(B) workers' compensation
(C) property insurance
(D) builders' risk insurance

**35.** A developed industrial property that includes a metal assembly building lost a quarter of its plants. Post-installation soil tests definitively link plant death to pre-existing soil conditions. While the project's bid instructions allowed bidders to perform soil tests before bid submittal, no soil tests were conducted. Which of the following is the most applicable, governing document that identifies who should pay for the corrective action?

(A) existing conditions plan; the landscape architect should pay because soil conditions should have been identified

(B) general conditions; the owner should pay for unforeseen conditions because it is an industrial property

(C) technical specifications; the contractor should pay because soil tests should have been conducted before plants were installed

(D) bid instructions; bidders should pay because soil testing was allowed prior to bid submittal

**36.** During construction, landscape architects are responsible for performing which of the following tasks?

(A) prepare site plans, layout plans, and grading and drainage plans

(B) coordinate consultant drawings

(C) organize drainage system details

(D) all of the above

**37.** Which of the following statements is NOT true?

(A) Both parties must have capacity for a contract to be valid.

(B) If breached, a void contract is legally binding.

(C) An unenforceable contract is generally valid, but not enforceable due to public policy or law.

(D) A minor is not legally responsible for contracts entered into.

**38.** While a project is under construction, payments from the owner to the landscape architect stop. To ensure final payments are received, the landscape architect must

I. use an independent party to verify the quantity of materials delivered or installed
II. submit an invoice by certified mail to the owner
III. file a lawsuit for breach of contract
IV. file a notice of *lis pendens* on the property title
V. place a lien on the property title

(A) I and II

(B) III and IV

(C) I, II, and III

(D) I, II, III, IV and V

39. During project's construction, a pedestrian slips and falls on a jobsite sidewalk designed by the landscape architect. The landscape architect is notified of the accident by the local police. To ensure payment for the pedestrian's injuries, the landscape architect should
   I. verify the accident location and site conditions using an independent party
   II. notify the liability insurance company
   III. notify the contractor
   IV. notify the project's property owner
   - (A) I and II
   - (B) III and IV
   - (C) I, II, and III
   - (D) I, II, III, and IV

40. How does retainage affect the contract value?
   - (A) It reduces the contract value.
   - (B) It increases the contract value.
   - (C) It has no impact on the contract value.
   - (D) It reduces the contract value when imposed, and then increases the value when paid.

41. To close out a new project, the best combination of tasks would be to
   - (A) assign a project number for tracking and create file folders for contracts, correspondence, codes, permits, and calculations
   - (B) use close-out software and assign follow-up tasks to administrative assistant
   - (C) create file folders for contract close-out correspondence, warranty phase inspections, and permit closeouts
   - (D) create file folders for annual tax returns, 401(K)s, pensions, and Social Security

42. A landscape architect designed a brightly colored sculpture that featured sharp metal edges to look like a play structure. The clients, who live in a residential neighborhood near an elementary school, placed the sculpture in their unfenced front yard, which increased their property's value. Regrettably, a child trespassing in the yard was injured while playing on the sculpture. Which of the following is the legal doctrine that holds the landowner liable for the child's injuries?
   - (A) attractive nuisance
   - (B) caveat emptor
   - (C) value by design
   - (D) proximate cause

## Construction Evaluation

**43.** Which of the following tasks and cost elements should be the basis for quoting a fee to a client with a project requiring several phases of construction?

    (A) plans, correspondence, codes, permits, and calculations to determine hourly rates

    (B) feasibility studies, design and construction documents, and estimates for post-construction services

    (C) preliminary concepts, final designs, and the construction phase services compiled for a lump sum fee

    (D) taxes, 401(K)s, pensions, and Social Security charged as part of overhead, then added to cost of direct expenses

**44.** Twenty-five percent of a project site's trees died, and undisputed test results showed a tree disease was at fault. Who is responsible for informing the landscape contractor and adjusting the landscaping contract amount?

    (A) the landscape architect

    (B) a professional forester

    (C) a plant pathologist

    (D) a terrestrial ecologist

**45.** Surveyors conduct which of the following tasks during construction?

    (A) mapping, legal descriptions, verification of earthwork quantities, measurement of ponds, and layouts of vertical and horizontal alignment

    (B) site inspections, submittals of products, and start-up instructions

    (C) safety instructions

    (D) supervision of contractor staff

**46.** Material testing firms perform all of the following during the construction phase of a project EXCEPT

    (A) verification of earthwork densities

    (B) sieve analyses

    (C) irrigation systems evaluations

    (D) slump and break tests

**47.** The main functions of the clerk of works do NOT include

    (A) verifying the quantities of delivered earthwork

    (B) logging and tracking visitors in and out of the jobsite

    (C) measuring stored products

    (D) supervising contractor staff

**48.** Agronomic soil testing is an important part of landscaping during project construction phase because it verifies

    (A) quantities of plant material
    (B) soil fertility
    (C) soil amendment performance
    (D) both B and C

**49.** Retainage, when applied to contract amounts, may be properly used by a project owner to

  I. hold funds for project or task completion
  II. correct defective work to increase the quality of the work completed
  III. improve cash flow during construction phase
  IV. fund counterclaims against a contractor

    (A) I
    (B) I and IV
    (C) II and III
    (D) I, II, and IV

**50.** Describing a site as "substantially complete" indicates that

    (A) a contractor's final payments have been received
    (B) the site is suitable for "move-in"
    (C) the contractor is released from contractual obligations
    (D) the project is finished

**51.** Private property restrictions include items listed in the title report that affect property use or improvements. The party most often responsible to read and show the property restrictions is the

    (A) professional land surveyor
    (B) owner
    (C) landscape architect
    (D) title company

**52.** In order to maintain irrigation system performance post-construction, the landscape architect would recommend a client do which of the following?

    (A) order a water audit
    (B) buy irrigation replacement parts that match the system's original design
    (C) set a water budget that reduces current irrigation application rates
    (D) both A and B

**53.** Post-occupancy evaluations (POE) are used to

(A) improve buildings and manage costs
(B) assess advantages and limitations of a design
(C) collect data by interviewing site users
(D) all of the above

**54.** A landscape architect wants to conduct a post-construction, citywide survey to determine if a site design used by the city's residents was successful. Which of the following should the landscape architect use to conduct the survey?

(A) volunteer sampling
(B) statistically valid random sampling
(C) self-selective sampling
(D) convenience sampling

**55.** The most important reference a landscape architect should use to evaluate plans for the landscaping design of a neighborhood park that is located in a high crime area would be

(A) IES standards
(B) QA/QC criteria
(C) CPTED guidelines
(D) IBC requirements

**56.** Before preparing a landscape construction bid, a landscape contractor should review a proposed project's construction documents. Construction documents usually include
I. working drawings
II. specifications
III. general conditions
IV. an agreement form
V. a punch list

(A) I and II
(B) III and IV
(C) II, IV, and V
(D) I, II, III, and IV

## Construction Practices

**57.** Best management practices for temporary soil erosion and sediment control are based on

(A) specific site conditions
(B) construction activities
(C) cost
(D) all of the above

**58.** To use federal funding on a project managed by a state or city, the specification for a contractor's performance would require

    (A) a Davis-Bacon prevailing wage scale

    (B) an indefinite delivery/indefinite quantity contract

    (C) a Federal Business Opportunities (FBO) listing

    (D) an advertisement in the *Federal Register*

**59.** An unregistered landscape architect designed a pergola for a client's private property in a state requiring such structures be designed by registered landscape architects. The structure initially appeared fine, but the footing did not have adequate steel reinforcement and was of an inadequate size to meet local codes. The structure eventually collapsed and injured a trespasser. The client was forced to remove the structure at a significant cost. The party most likely responsible for all damages, including the cost to remove the structure, would be the

    (A) client

    (B) unregistered landscape architect

    (C) property liability insurance company

    (D) injured trespasser

**60.** The Architect's Supplemental Instruction is a

    (A) Request for Interpretation response

    (B) contract change to clarify errors

    (C) list of additional tasks the landscape architect is required to perform

    (D) subset of the federal Modification of Contract Form 30

**61.** Who would most likely prepare a soils test report to determine the soil structure, nutrients, minerals, acidity, and minor element components of wetland soil?

    (A) agronomist

    (B) landscape contractor

    (C) hydrologist

    (D) biologist

**62.** A large plant nursery adjacent to an airport needs to be acquired for a proposed airport terminal expansion project. The airport landscape architect has been asked to advise the airport authority of the value of the nursery operation. The financial value (in dollars per square foot of land area) of the nursery would be established by the

    (A) age, size, spacing, number, condition, and species of plants with factors for market demand, multiplied by a price for the plants when the nursery would close

    (B) most recent full year sales from the nursery divided by the nursery's size

    (C) increased airport revenues before and after the expansion, prorated for the size of the nursery

    (D) market value of the land

## Problems

**63.** Which actions will a biologist typically perform during project construction phase?
  I. map wetland plant species within a transect
  II. monitor success of biological mitigation
  III. measure vegetation plant canopy cover
  IV. provide instructions for handling chemicals
  V. verify water level fluctuation in wetlands

  (A) I and II
  (B) III and IV
  (C) I, III, and V
  (D) II, IV, and V

**64.** The specific procedure to pressure test an irrigation main during construction would be found in the

  (A) General Specifications for verification of quantities and measurement sections
  (B) technical sections for submittals of products and start-up instructions
  (C) safety instructions in local codes
  (D) contractor performance section in technical specifications

**65.** The testing requirements for irrigation system backflow prevention device would be found in the

  (A) verification of quantities general specifications
  (B) technical sections for submittals of products and start-up instructions
  (C) local or state health codes
  (D) contractor performance section of technical specifications

**66.** Requirements for site soil tests would be found in

  (A) general specifications
  (B) product submittal technical sections
  (C) safety instructions in local codes
  (D) contractor performance section of technical specifications

**67.** Post-construction landscape ordinances focus on

  (A) tree preservation
  (B) individual site plans
  (C) controlling stormwater runoff
  (D) all of the above

**68.** A landscape architect is working on a green building project and is documenting water efficiency so the project may earn points towards certification. Which of the following would provide criteria and standards for project environmental performance?

(A) Leadership in Energy and Environmental Design (LEED®)
(B) Construction Specifications Institute (CSI)
(C) National Association of Office and Industrial Parks (NAOIP)
(D) Urban Land Institute (ULI)

**69.** Which of the following would a landscape architect recommend as a sustainable, best practice recommendation?

(A) growing bamboo species in tropical coastal regions
(B) storing biogenetic experimentation records in university libraries
(C) using nonnative vegetation for site landscaping
(D) encouraging tissue cultures for ornamental horticultural use

**70.** Which of the following are NOT examples of sustainable construction practices?

I. using bio-based hydraulic fluids
II. disposing of inert solids
III. creating a construction waste and debris management plan
IV. treating lumber with CCA
V. utilizing post-consumer aluminum

(A) I and III
(B) II and IV
(C) I, II, and V
(D) II, III, and IV

# Solutions

1. C
2. A
3. D
4. D
5. D
6. D
7. C
8. D
9. D
10. C
11. B
12. D
13. C
14. B
15. C
16. D
17. C
18. A
19. A
20. D
21. D
22. B
23. A
24. A
25. A
26. A
27. C
28. C
29. D
30. C
31. B
32. D
33. B
34. A
35. C
36. D
37. B
38. C
39. D
40. C
41. C
42. A
43. B
44. A
45. A
46. C
47. D
48. C
49. A
50. B
51. A
52. D
53. C
54. B
55. C
56. D
57. D
58. A
59. A
60. B
61. A
62. A
63. C
64. D
65. C
66. D
67. C
68. A
69. A
70. B

# Solutions

## Communication

**1.** Consensus decision making is a process used to discuss a group's key individual concerns to ultimately achieve a defined purpose or outcome. It does not limit the number of applicable participants; rather all interested parties are encouraged to participate. Consensus decision making utilizes a facilitator to ensure each participant's viewpoint is heard and recorded, as well as to lead the group in open discussions about individual comments. A proposal is formed based on the group's discussion; however, if consensus on the proposal is not immediately achieved, concerns are identified and addressed, the proposal is amended, and another round of discussion is held until a group consensus is attained. In this process, comments, opinions, or ideas not supported by the group's majority are discarded.

*The answer is (C).*

**2.** A charette is an intensive, multi-day process designed to bring people from different subgroups into consensus in a short amount of time. It is often applied during development, design, and planning processes that will have significant community impact. The National Charrette Institute states a charrette should last between four to seven days, not one day, depending on the difficulty of the project. Because charrettes need detailed preparation to be implemented effectively, they require significant resources to collect and analyze data, photograph the site, contact and engage the community and stakeholders, and locate an appropriate space for public meetings. The charrette should consist of a design team consisting of diverse professionals who are capable of considering all relevant, public feedback. However, the design team does not unilaterally author a final plan. Instead, through a series of short "feedback loops" that are used to present the plans to the community, plans are reviewed and then critiqued by the community. The feedback loops continue as the team refines and re-presents alternate plans until a final plan is decided upon.

*The answer is (A).*

**3.** To reach a consensus about a long range regional planning proposal, a planning commission may interview key community informants and stakeholders, distribute a mail-out/mail-in survey to a random sample of community residents, administer a telephone survey to a random sample of community residents, or provide a link to a questionnaire and/or survey on the community's internet homepage.

Conducting interviews helps identify and define issues for surveys, and it is always best to use at least two types of survey methods. Using more than one survey method helps to widen possible participation and to gather a more diverse collection of responses. Using websites to administer questionnaires and/or surveys is also a growing method of acquiring participation in regional planning.

*The answer is (D).*

**4.** The purpose of taking minutes is to officially record meeting proceedings, note which tasks are assigned to whom, and act as the official record of the meeting.

*The answer is (D).*

**5.** A landscape contractor is responsible for all site construction work as identified by the Construction Documents; estimating a bid price based on physical analysis of the site and related technical reports; determining the appropriate construction strategy by assessing site access, magnitude of work and materials needed, and time available; and submitting mechanics lien affidavits before final payment may be made.

*The answer is (D).*

**6.** All given consequences are possible. Tort liability is possible because water leaving one site and entering another is a form of direct trespass. The subconsultant civil engineer could be required to pay the property damage claim if his or her performance played some role in causing the water to leave the site. A code violation could result from the water discharge, if local code requires a storm event to be retained (for example, a 100-year event). If the landscape architect had a duty to retain stormwater and failed, a breach of contract or negligence claim from the property owner to either the landscape architect or the civil engineer (or both) could occur.

*The answer is (D).*

**7.** The county would be liable since its design and project caused the damage, irregardless of whether or not the pipe was designed by registered staff. The county is also liable even if it is insured by a professional liability insurance company. In instances where the flow of a natural stream is split near an already developed residential area, private professionals with insurance should be used instead of a public agency's in-house staff. If the county had used a private consultant with professional liability coverage to design the project, the consulting firm, not the county, would have been liable for the property damage claims.

*The answer is (C).*

**8.** Depending on the scale and complexity of a project, utility plans will include stormwater drainage (i.e., surface and subsurface conveyance systems), and sanitary sewer and septic systems. Utility plans also include (but not listed among answer choices) water distribution (i.e., potable drinking, irrigation, reclaimed water, and fire control), electrical layout, buried cables (i.e., telephone lines, cable TV, fiber optic transmissions, etc.), pipes for chemicals, steam and heat lines, and fuel transmission pipelines for natural gas and petroleum. A utility plan would not include paved areas, terraces, and walls.

*The answer is (D).*

**9.** Because the project is in the beginning stages of design, the landscape architect should conduct a project kickoff meeting followed by sending out minutes. The landscape architect can use the kickoff meeting to demonstrate how the project will be managed and coordinated, and which design team member will perform what task and when.

Option A is incorrect because while a teleconference is an acceptable *method* for conducting a meeting, it does not specify what *type* of meeting the landscape architect should conduct. Option B is incorrect because the pre-submittal conference would occur before the landscape architect and team are selected. Option C is incorrect because the post-construction conference occurs after the design is completed.

***The answer is (D).***

**10.** The best method to create a balanced workgroup is to have select members of the existing workgroup separately interview candidates, and then compare notes before hiring new members. This method allows members to assess a candidate's communication, personality, leadership, and management styles. By comparing multiple member notes taken during the interview, the firm can determine a more objective view of each candidate's strengths and weaknesses, as well as assess overall fit with the current workgroup.

Personality tests and management leadership style assessments can provide useful information; however, each method requires making decisions after test results are available, and the administration of testing prior to hiring might be governed by employment regulations. Regular workgroup meetings can create positive small group dynamics and foster team building. However, these meeting are typically for workgroup members only, and thus, would take place after candidates are hired. They are not an effective means to assemble a workgroup.

***The answer is (C).***

**11.** The city hired the landscape architect as part of its downtown redevelopment plan to help retain businesses that are contemplating relocation. Therefore, the landscape architect's first step in organizing the project team should be to recruit an economist who can conduct a market study to survey businesses and assess their competition and customers. Without a market study, it would be difficult to determine what factors are influencing businesses to relocate, and for the project team to determine an appropriate downtown redevelopment design.

While a site analysis might confirm the reasons behind the variance of tree sizes (e.g., differences in sunlight availability), the cause and effect of the street trees' size on the businesses is not established in the problem statement and can only be used to speculate why businesses want to relocate; therefore, option A is incorrect. Option C is incorrect because site design measures controlled by landscape architects *do* affect businesses by either attracting or detracting customers. The landscape architect could help retain businesses by implementing a design that would increase pedestrian comfort, parking convenience, and business sign visibility. There is not enough information given in the problem statement to determine whether or not the project architect would be in a better position than the landscape architect to organize the project team; therefore, option D is incorrect.

***The answer is (B).***

**12.** In 1965, Bruce Tuckman proposed a four-stage model of group dynamics. The four phases included forming, storming, norming, and performing. The first stage in a group's development, or dynamic, is *forming*. During this stage, the team meets, learns about project objectives, and agrees on ways to accomplish project tasks. The second phase, *storming*, is categorized by conflict as members compete to have their differing ideas considered. The storming phase is an important step in group dynamics because it allows group members to test limits, find out how the team works under pressure, and determine who may be best for what tasks. Skipping the storming stage, or seeking to minimize conflict rather than resolve it, can create less than optimal group performance results or even lead to failure factors, such as members bowing out, or only a few carrying the group effort. During the third phase, *norming*, members develop work techniques that foster teamwork, trust, and motivation. In the fourth stage, *performing*, group members work interdependently, with high levels of motivation and low levels of inappropriate conflict until the task is completed. Differing ideas are expected and used to fuel creativity.

The problem statement indicates that conflict has developed amongst the project team as members are fighting to have their own ideas considered. While conflict can arise at any stage, it is most likely to occur during the storming stage.

***The answer is (D).***

**13.** The consultant and the owner are the parties involved in an agreement for professional services.

A tenant and property owner would use a lease agreement. A contractor and subcontractor, as well as an owner and contractor, would use construction agreements.

***The answer is (C).***

**14.** Agendas should be distributed before a meeting takes place so that participants know what topics will be discussed and can prepare accordingly. They should not be handed out the day of the meeting.

Agendas should specify the meeting date, time, and location, as well as the purpose of the meeting. They are prioritized so that the most important items are discussed first, and are task orientated so that participants are clear about discussion topics.

***The answer is (B).***

## Standards of Practice

**15.** Inflating cost estimates used for fee calculation is a breach of ethics because it places the professional's financial interests ahead of the client's.

Disclosing financial interests would actually correct or avoid an ethical breach. Respecting a confidentiality request from a client is expected in all cases; furthermore, confidentiality is usually a contractual requirement. The problem statement does not indicate that the confidence disclosure is associated with any violation of public regulations—which is the one exception that allows disclosure of confidential client information. Maintaining social relationships with private clients while delivering professional services under contract is generally acceptable, especially in small communities, and option (D) does not specify any ethical concern being at issue in the social relationship with the client.

***The answer is (C).***

# Solutions

**16.** The critical path method (CPM) would be used to estimate a project's shortest completion time by analyzing only essential, interconnected activities. CPM is a project management tool used to manage a project's schedule. It provides a graphical illustration of a project, predicts the approximate time required to complete a project, and shows which tasks are essential to maintain a project's schedule versus tasks that are not. By evaluating the starting and ending time for each activity, CPM determines which activities are critical to a project's completion (known as the critical path), and ensures that noncritical activities do not interfere with critical ones.

Value engineering (VE) employs a multi-step job plan to analyze project requirements so that over the life of a project, essential job functions are achieved at their lowest costs. Work breakdown structure (WBS) uses a hierarchical tree structure to define and organize 100% of a project's scope (i.e., both a project's essential and nonessential activities). The project management plan (PMP) is a document used to record all key project and management factors (including nonessential tasks), and is updated throughout the life of a project. It includes project goals, technical requirements, schedules, budgets, and management programs.

*The answer is (D).*

**17.** The American Society of Landscape Architects (ASLA), in their *Code of Professional Ethics*, states that a landscape architect having reasonable belief and information that another landscape architect has violated an ethical code, must report such information to the appropriate committee. However, because reporting such information seriously questions the reported landscape architect's professional integrity and may provide cause for legal action against the reporter, the landscape architect should seek counsel from a legal advisor before reporting the suspected violation. In many cases, if the report is done in good faith, jurisdictions will often protect against libel or slander actions.

*The answer is (C).*

**18.** The Council of Landscape Architectural Registration Boards' (CLARB's) *Rules of Professional Conduct* state that a landscape architect may not sign or seal drawings, specifications, reports, or other professional work without direct professional knowledge or supervisory control. Landscape architects are permitted to use professional work prepared by consultants who are registered in the project's jurisdiction, if the landscape architect signing the document has reviewed the work, coordinated its preparations, and is willing to be responsible for the work's accuracy.

Landscape architects are permitted to offer gifts of nominal value (such as reasonable hospitality or entertainment), but they are not allowed to offer gifts of considerable value in order to sway an existing or prospective client's judgment. When making public statements about landscape architecture, they must disclose any compensation received for making such statements, and when acting as the interpreter of contract documents, they are to judge contract performance, but favor neither contract party.

*The answer is (A).*

# LARE Review, Section 1 Sample Exam

**19.** Wetlands are protected ecosystems and filling one most likely violates regional codes and regulations. The documents ASLA *Code of Environmental Ethics* and CLARB *Rules of Professional Conduct* require landscape architects to report any actions that violate state laws or regulations to the appropriate jurisdiction.

A landscape architect is able to ethically breach a client's confidentiality when the client has violated public regulations. If the landscape architect chose to conceal the information, the landscape architect could be held liable depending on the agency's enforcement policies. There is not enough information provided to know if the landscape architect should terminate services with the client. Termination is only required when the landscape architect reasonably believes that the client will continue to violate laws or regulations and disregard his or her advice. In such cases, the landscape architect is not liable to the client for terminating services.

*The answer is (A).*

**20.** To negotiate and prepare client/landscape architect precontract agreements, CLARB and the Landscape Architectural Registration Boards Foundation in their publication *The Road to Licensure and Beyond*, state that a landscape architect should elicit the client's needs and intentions for the project; identify relevant laws, rules, and regulations; coordinate and conduct field investigations; prepare site inventories (e.g., cultural, natural, and visual systems); and formulate project guidelines (e.g., the numbers, sizes, relationships, and functions of elements). Though not listed as answer options, when working on precontract agreements, landscape architects should also prepare preliminary budget estimates and collect site spe- cific data (e.g., demographics, infrastructures, etc.).

*The answer is (D).*

**21.** A government agency seeking to notify consultants or vendors of a project opportunity would list the project on the Federal Business Opportunities (FBO), or FedBizOpps. In 2002, FBO replaced the Commerce Business Daily (CBD), or CBD*net*, as the online, single government point-of-entry for federal project opportunities over $25,000. The FBO allows government buyers to publicize their business opportunities, and allows consulting firms or commercial vendors to search, monitor, and retrieve opportunities posted by the federal government. The FBO can be found at www.fedbizopps.gov. The *Federal Register* is published by the Office of the Federal Register, National Archives and Records Administration, and is the official publication for government laws and contracts. The *Federal Jobs Digest* is an employment newspaper that focuses on job vacancies and federal hiring. It would not be used to advertise a consulting opportunity over $25,000.

*The answer is (D).*

**22.** A city's specifications and requirements for fence height, minimum lots widths, and minimum lot size would be found in the regulations titled Development Criteria or Zoning Standards. The other answer choices given (Contracting Requirements, City Charter, and Resolutions) do not include regulations on height and bulk. Resolutions (similar to ordinances) refer to the document or the action taken by the jurisdiction to pass a code or regulation.

*The answer is (B).*

**23.** Project management software would most likely be necessary to track a multi-year, multi-million dollar project's schedule and cash flow. Project management software, such as Primavera®, enables professionals to organize and manage resources, compile and arrange task lists to meet deadlines, allocate schedules, identify early warning of when the project schedule or budget is at risk, record information about a project's actual and planned progress, and account for project dependencies.

Wall charts, Gantt charts, and a list of milestone dates are all project tracking and scheduling techniques, but are more appropriate for small or simple projects. Wall charts are displayed on the landscape architect's wall to provide a highly visible account for the work flow of the project team. Gantt charts, a type of bar chart, track a project's schedule by listing the timeline across the top of the chart and tasks to the left of the chart. Lines are used to indicate the starting and stopping point for each activity. Milestone lists merely log project tasks and the projected dates for each task's completion.

*The answer is (A).*

**24.** Landscape architects have a duty to maintain the administrative affairs of their clients' projects. Therefore, when starting a new project, they should first assign a project tracking number and create contract and correspondence file folders. Folders for codes, permits, and calculations should be created as well. Coordinating with consultants or design team members, and preparing statements of estimated construction costs are tasks that occur throughout the design process. Reviewing shop drawings and submittals would be performed as part of the landscape architect's construction administration duties.

*The answer is (A).*

**25.** The construction administration coordinator would be most likely to prepare a daily log of Requests for Information (RFIs), Architect's Supplemental Instructions (ASIs), payment requests, shop drawings, and change orders at the direction of the project manager or professional. The clerk of works and jobsite superintendents are not normally responsible for the tasks listed. The project manager would be responsible for overseeing, but not maintaining the daily log of RFIs, ASIs, payment requests, shop drawings, and change orders.

*The answer is (A).*

**26.** A landscape architect would be responsible for schedule delays caused by periodic site visits and/or reviews of specified technical submittals for the site's irrigation system. All other answer choices contain tasks or situations that an owner would be responsible for.

*The answer is (A).*

**27.** Based on the information provided in the problem statement, the landscape architect could face an allegation of gross negligence, a wrongful death claim, and a breach of contract claim from the property owner. There is not enough information in the problem statement to know if there was a local code violation.

Gross negligence is applicable because the landscape architect failed to act when information about a faulty product was known. A wrongful death claim is possible because the death was caused by the landscape architect's lack of action, even though there was no direct intention to kill the third party. (However, the landscape architect must be deemed negligent or strictly liable for the third party's death before a wrongful death claim may be made.)

A breach of contract may also result from the landscape architect's failure to protect the owner and the public from danger. Professionals, such as consultants, contractors, and landscape architects operate under a code of professional ethics, as well as state licensing requirements, in order to avoid harming or putting the public at risk.

*The answer is (C).*

**28.** A backcharge is the adjustment method by which a contractor charges the responsible party for repeating a task or correcting a sequential step, and would be used to adjust the total cost to fix the foundation's elevation.

The other answer choices are similar sounding terms that apply to banking (overdraft), fire suppression (backdraft), and pressurized gas mechanical systems (overcharge).

*The answer is (C).*

**29.** A bid price encompasses the landscape contractor's cost to prepare the site, clear the site, furnish and install all specified materials, provide the necessary equipment and labor crews to complete the work on time, and the operation's overhead expenses and profit. Most bid prices also allow for unforeseen contingencies that can range from an additional 5% to 20% added to the quoted costs.

*The answer is (D).*

**30.** The Construction Specification Institute (CSI) is a national organization that maintains the standards, language, and formats of construction documents. CSI's MasterFormat™ is an industry tool that organizes construction specification requirements and documents. The major source of construction specifications is found in MasterFormat division 02, Existing Conditions, with includes specifications for surveying, site decontamination, and site remediation, to name a few. Division 00 contains specifications for procurement and contracting requirements. Division 01 contains specifications for general requirements, and division 03 lists specifications for concrete. For more information about CSI or MasterFormat, go to www.csinet.org.

*The answer is (C).*

## Contract Administration

**31.** The Construction Change Directive, based on AIA document G714™, and the Change Order, based on AIA form G701™, are two forms that may be used to change the work, the contract time limit, or the contract amount (or sum).

The Architect's Supplemental Instruction based on AIA document G710™ may be used to make minor changes to the contract, but it cannot adjust contract time or contract amount. The General Conditions of the Contract for Construction, based on AIA document A201™, is used to record the rights, responsibilities, and relationships of the owner, contractor, and landscape architect.

*The answer is (B).*

**32.** Bid addenda may be used to change a bid date, to revise bid documents, or to seek information when a Request for Information (RFI) is submitted. They are often used to change the time, scope, or cost estimate of a project. However, bid addenda are not appropriate to use after a contract is awarded; they may only be used before a contract is awarded. After a contract is awarded, changes are made using the Construction Change Directive, Architect's Supplemental Instruction, or Change Order forms.

*The answer is (D).*

**33.** A breach of contract occurs when one side of a party fails to fulfill the specified terms of a signed agreement. The problem statement indicates that the project is operating under specified time limits (i.e., "time is of the essence"); therefore, failing to complete the project within the allowed timeframe is the only answer choice that constitutes a breach of contract.

While the problem statement notes the contractor signed a nondisclosure agreement, it does not specify the nature of that agreement, so there is not enough information to know if option (A) is correct. In many cases, contractors are actually required to disclose project financials to a surety company or lender, and project costs may be disclosed to cities to establish building plan permit and reviewing costs. Disclosing information that is potentially damaging to the owner does not necessarily constitute a contract breach (unless the disclosed information was outlined in the nondisclosure agreement). For example, a contractor may be obligated to disclose potentially damaging information to the owner if required by law or court order; there is not enough information in the problem statement to determine if the disclosed information is a breach of contract.

*The answer is (C).*

**34.** General liability insurance is a basic type of commercial insurance that is limited to a third party's property damage or personal injury claims. Workers' compensation, also known in some states as industrial insurance, covers an employee's work-related personal injury or illness claims. Property insurance protects against flood, earthquake, fire damage, or theft against a property. Builders' risk insurance is a subset of property insurance that protects against damage to buildings that are under construction.

*The answer is (A).*

**35.** The technical specifications are the most applicable, governing document to determine who should pay for the corrective action. The contractor will be responsible to pay for the corrective action because he or she should have first conducted existing site soil tests of the planting areas, and these tests should have been reviewed by the landscape architect before plants were ordered, delivered, and installed. The plant mortality rate was linked to existing soil conditions indicating that the contractor did not perform a pre-installation soils test.

An existing conditions plan is usually a reproduction of a site survey plan that shows total acres, topography, existing structures and vegetation, and so forth. It does not note responsibility for corrective action payment; therefore, option (A) is incorrect. Option (B) uses the problem statement's extra information about the site's industrial use to distract the reader to erroneously conclude that the presence of metals is related to the dead plants. While plant death can be caused by the presence of metals in soil, there is not enough information provided by the problem statement to link it to the plants' death. Option (D) is incorrect because while the soil conditions were potentially knowable, as bidders could perform soils tests prior to submitting bids, the bid instructions would not state who should pay for corrective action.

*The answer is (C).*

**36.** During construction, landscape architects will prepare site plans, layout plans, and grading and drainage plans; coordinate consultant drawings; and organize drainage system details. CLARB and the Landscape Architectural Registration Boards Foundation gives a complete list of tasks performed by landscape architects under the Construction Documents in their publication, *The Road to Licensure and Beyond*.

*The answer is (D).*

**37.** If breached, a void contract would not be legally binding because the contract was never valid. A common example of a voided contract is a contract signed under duress. The contract would not be valid because the parties were not in mutual agreement. For a contract to be valid, both parties must not only be in agreement, but they both must also have capacity. Legally speaking, capacity is the ability to know and understand the terms of the contract. Most states consider minors (persons under the age of eighteen) to lack the capacity to enter into a contract. Therefore, in most cases a minor is not legally responsible for contracts entered into. Lack of capacity also applies to mentally disabled persons and persons who are intoxicated. An unenforceable contract is generally valid, but not enforceable due to public policy or law. For example, a contract requiring a person to commit a crime would be unenforceable.

*The answer is (B).*

**38.** To ensure final payment is received when payments from an owner stop during construction, the landscape architect must use an independent party to verify quantities of materials or services delivered or installed, submit an invoice by certified mail to the owner, file a lawsuit for a breach of contract, place a lien on the property title, and file a notice of *lis pendens* (pending litigation) on the property title.

*The answer is (D).*

**39.** When a professional is notified of a jobsite incident, it is important to first collect information in order to later determine if any aspect of the professional's work was at issue. Verification of the accident location and site conditions should be done by an independent party. Usually, the liability insurance company will advise this step, or collect the incident information when notified. The contractor must be notified since the contractor is responsible for project site safety during construction. The property owner also must be notified because a personal injury claim could eventually include the owner.

*The answer is (D).*

**40.** Retainage has no impact on the contract value. The periodic or monthly payment requests/amounts might be reduced for retainage, but the overall contract value would not increase or decrease.

*The answer is (C).*

**41.** To close out a new project, one should create file folders for contract closeout correspondence, warranty phase inspections, and permit closeouts. All other options (i.e., hire staff or creating other files) are not as directly tied to project closeout procedures.

*The answer is (C).*

**42.** The attractive nuisance doctrine states that a landowner may be held liable for a child's injuries if the injuries are caused by a hazardous object or property condition that is likely to attract children. The problem statement indicates that the sculpture has bright colors, looks like a play structure, and is placed in a client's unfenced front yard, which is close to an elementary school. Because children are unable to assess an object's potential risk, landowners have a duty to exercise reasonable care to eliminate danger or to protect children from accessible objects on their property.

None of the other answer choices are legal doctrines. Caveat emptor means "let the buyer beware" and is associated with concealed conditions for property purchase. Value by design is a concept describing a property's financial value that stems from qualitative improvements. Proximate cause is an event related to the last negligent action that occurs prior to an injury, and that without which, the injury would not have occurred.

*The answer is (A).*

## Construction Evaluation

**43.** A landscape architect should use a feasibility study for time and materials, design and construction documents to determine a lump sum fee or a percentage of the construction cost, and estimates of post-construction services for time and materials to determine a quote for a client whose project will require several phases of construction. Master planning and schematic design are also cost elements that should be factored into a project's fee.

Organizing plans, correspondence, and permits, and estimating taxes, pensions, and Social Security are actions related to file structure, not fees. A lump sum fee for the preliminary concept, final design, and the construction phase is incomplete because it leaves out construction documents fee, and is not the most complete sequential description.

*The answer is (B).*

**44.** In 49 states and the District of Columbia, a project site's landscape architect is recognized as responsible for informing the landscape contractor that trees have died, and to adjust the contract amount for the landscape planting. Arborists, foresters, or plant pathologists might be able to determine a tree's cause of death, but they would not be the best arbiters of contractual issues.

*The answer is (A).*

**45.** Surveyors provide mapping, legal descriptions, verification of earthwork quantities, measurement of ponds, and layouts of vertical and horizontal alignment. Site inspections, submittals of products, start-up and safety instructions, and the supervision of contractor staff are conducted by the project's contractor.

*The answer is (A).*

**46.** Material testing firms perform a number of tasks during construction, such as verifying earthwork densities, conducting sieve analyses to measure particle sizes in granular soil or rock material, and performing slump and break tests to check concrete strength. They do not typically evaluate irrigation systems. An irrigation system's evaluation is performed by the landscape architect, or an irrigation consultant assisting the landscape architect.

*The answer is (C).*

**47.** The clerk of works, also known as the site inspector, verifies the quantities of delivered earthwork, measures stored products, and logs and tracks visitors in and out of the jobsite. A clerk of works may meet with contractor staff while carrying out visual inspections of the works, but contractor staff supervision is a project manager or supervisor task.

*The answer is (D).*

**48.** Conducting agronomic soil testing during a project's construction phase is important because it verifies soil amendment performance and soil fertility to ensure soil is more productive for plant growth. Verifying plant material quantities is not related to agronomy.

*The answer is (D).*

**49.** Retainage is a contracted portion or a percentage of payments due for work completed. The amount is retained by the owner until a project is finished. An improper use of retainage would be to correct defective work using the withheld funds, or to use the funds to improve cash flow during the construction phase. Retainage should not be used in counterclaims against a contractor, or in claims unrelated to the retainage.

*The answer is (A).*

**50.** Substantial completion is a term used to describe work that is in "move-in" condition, meaning that the owner may occupy or use the site for its intended purpose. When a site is substantially complete, it is not finished. Rather, at this time, a punch list is created to catalog all items needing to be completed or corrected. Finally, a contractor would not receive final payment until all mechanics liens are certified as being paid, at which point he or she is released from all contractual obligations.

*The answer is (B).*

**51.** The professional land surveyor is most frequently the member of the design team to read and also show the property restrictions. The owner may know of the restrictions, but not be able to fully understand how a restriction affects a project's proposed use or improvements. The title company staff is responsible to provide the restrictions, typically to the party who paid for the title report. The landscape architect could become liable for any restrictions that exist, but are not properly shown, and the surveyor is better trained to read and show the range of private restrictions (e.g., reservations, easements, encroachments, latent parcels, or rights-of-way) affecting a property.

*The answer is (A).*

**52.** To maintain an irrigation system's performance post-construction, the landscape architect would recommend the client order a water audit, and that replacement parts match the system's original design. A water audit (or water-use evaluation) identifies where excess water is being used and can help determine practices to reduce excess water consumption. The Irrigation Association® publishes irrigation water audit performance standards. Buying replacement parts that match a system's original design ensures that the system will function as it was designed to.

Option C is incorrect because conserving water may be necessary if it is needed for other purposes, such as for aquifer or groundwater recharging. Therefore, setting a water budget to reduce water application may jeopardize the health of the landscaping, or negatively impact certain types of soil. For example, many plants need regular watering, and cracking or fissures can occur in soil when it begins to dry out.

*The answer is (D).*

**53.** Post-occupancy evaluations (POEs) are often used to determine how well a design performs post-construction. POEs assess the advantages and limitations of a design, and collect data about the design through observation and interviews with the site users to gage user design satisfaction. POEs provide feedback existing conditions, propose solutions to existing problems, and help produce design guidelines for future projects. POEs can be useful tools to improve future building designs and costs, as well as increase user comfort and satisfaction.

*The answer is (D).*

**54.** The landscape architect should use statistically valid random sampling to conduct the citywide survey of residents. Key to this problem is the statement that the landscape architect is trying to determine if the design was successful at the citywide scale. With random sampling, each member of a population has an equal probability of being selected; therefore, results from the sample can be applied to the general population. Volunteer, self-selective, and convenience sampling are nonprobability based sampling methods, meaning results cannot be reliably applied to the general population. The advantage of random sample probability methods is that the sampling error is known so that results may be reported plus or minus the sampling error. The sampling error, or the degree of bias and accuracy for the nonprobability based methods, is unknown.

*The answer is (B).*

**55.** An evaluation of the plans for the landscaping design of a neighborhood park located in a high crime area would reference crime prevention through environmental design (CPTED) guidelines. CPTED guidelines are developed by law enforcement and design professionals to help make public facilities and sites safe by designing physical environments to be perceived by would-be criminals as a risky place to commit a crime.

The other answer options are incorrect. The Illuminations Engineering Society (IES) publishes lighting level standards and there is not enough information presented about the park's nighttime use to know if the landscape architect should reference IES standards. Referencing quality assurance/quality control (QA/QC) criteria may be relevant to ensure the landscaping design adheres to quality standards; however, because the park is located in a high crime area, it is more important for the landscape architect to reference CPTED guidelines. The *International Building Code* (IBC) is used by several jurisdictions, but it does not address design techniques to mitigate crime.

*The answer is (C).*

**56.** In order to prepare an accurate bid, a landscape contractor must thoroughly review the construction documents. Construction documents are usually divided into four categories: working drawings (scaled graphic plans representing the proposed site development), specifications (written descriptions of desired work, methods to be used, performance requirements, and quality standards), general conditions (contract requirements including insurance coverage, field change orders, or other administrative duties), and an agreement form (a legally binding document between the owner and the contractor containing a complete list of bid items). A punch list is created by the owner at the end of a project and includes tasks that need to be repaired or completed by the contractor.

*The answer is (D).*

## Construction Practices

**57.** Best management practices (BMPs) for temporary soil erosion and sediment controls are based on specific site conditions, construction activities, and cost. The BMPs mentioned in the problem statement are based on specific site conditions or construction activities such as stabilizing disturbed areas, retaining sediment onsite, and protecting slopes and channels.

*The answer is (D).*

**58.** To use federal funding on a project managed by a state or city, the specification for a contractor's performance would require compliance with a prevailing wage scale. The prevailing wage scale was established by the Davis-Bacon Act of 1931, which requires all federal construction contracts, and most federally assisted construction contracts over $2000, to pay workers local prevailing wages unless specifically waived by the enabling legislation.

The Federal Business Opportunities (FBO) and the *Federal Register* are publications used to list federal contracts and laws, and the indefinite delivery/indefinite quantity contract is a type of contract.

*The answer is (A).*

# Solutions

**59.** The client hired an unregistered landscape architect to do a job that required a registered landscape architect. Therefore, the client would be responsible for all damages, including the cost to remove the structure. There is not enough information provided in the problem statement to know if the unregistered landscape architect misled the client about his or her registered status; therefore option (B) is incorrect.

Option (C) is incorrect because property liability insurance rarely covers damages when a structure does not meet local codes or conform to state regulations. Option (D) is incorrect, as the injured trespasser would not be liable because property owners are required to maintain property in safe condition for both invited guests and trespassers.

*The answer is (A).*

**60.** The Architect's Supplemental Instruction (ASI) is based on AIA document G710. It is used to clearup errors, inconsistencies, omissions, and apparent discrepancies discovered by the project owner or contractor after an agreement has been signed. It is also used to change the contract conditions, or to request minor changes in the work as long as they do not change contract time or contract cost.

The ASI is not a list of additional tasks the architect must perform, nor is it a subset of the federal Modification of Contract Form 30 (also called an Amendment of Solicitation), which is used with federal projects to change a project's work, time, or sum. The Request for Interpretation (RFI) is used to exchange project information or details.

*The answer is (B).*

**61.** An agronomist is a soil scientist and is responsible for preparing a soils test report that includes the soil structure, nutrients, minerals, acidity, and the minor element components of wetland soil. The landscape contractor might collect a soil sample and deliver it to the agronomist; however, the landscape contractor is not qualified to analyze soils and prepare reports. Hydrologists assess subsurface or surface water flows, as well as the effects of water in soils, such as infiltration rates, erosion, and so forth. Biologists study general living systems, including wetlands, but are not necessarily experts on soil composition.

*The answer is (A).*

**62.** All of the answer choices provide different methods to reach dollars per square foot for the value of the nursery real estate, but only option (A) would establish a property's financial value using services provided by a landscape architect. Landscape architects regularly give informed opinions based on the age, size, spacing, number, condition, and species of plants with factors for market demand. The anticipated price for plants at the time of the nursery's closure, based on the best available information, can be expressed in a value in dollars per square foot for the evaluation of offers and negotiations. Plants that could not be moved (e.g., they are too big, too closely spaced, or not in conformance with grades and standards) should be shown as a cost to remove, rather than a potential source of revenue. Opinions about prior year nursery sales, airport revenues, and land values are best left to accountants, airport finance experts, and real estate professionals.

*The answer is (A).*

# LARE Review, Section 1 Sample Exam

**63.** The responsibilities of the biologist range greatly during the construction phase. Biologists may be called to clarify or make the landscape architect aware of a site's biological issues or constraints, or to provide a complete description of the biological impacts of the site design. Biologists are also responsible for the mapping of wetland plant transects, water level fluctuation measurements, and plant canopy cover measurements.

While biologists *are* responsible for monitoring the success of any biological mitigation that was a condition of construction, this monitoring takes place post-construction, not during construction. Biologists do not provide instructions for handling chemicals.

*The answer is (C).*

**64.** During construction, the pressure test procedures of an irrigation main would be found in the contractor performance section in the technical specifications. General specifications, safety codes, and product or start-up sections are not related to the pressure test, which is a performance specification.

*The answer is (D).*

**65.** Backflow prevention devices are connected to an irrigation system during the construction phase of a project to prevent cross-contamination of potable water systems. Because backflow prevention devices are installed to protect the safety of drinking water, testing requirements would be found in local or state health codes. General specifications, product or start-up instructions, and the contractor performance section of technical specifications would not contain backflow prevention device testing requirements.

*The answer is (C).*

**66.** The contractor is responsible for ensuring soil tests are conducted before any landscaping is installed. Therefore, soil test requirements would be located in the contractor performance section of the technical specifications. General specifications, product submissions, or safety instruction sections are not related to soil testing. Soil testing might be included in the quality assurance section of specifications (which was not offered as an answer choice), but the detailed requirements of the soil tests would be in the performance section.

*The answer is (D).*

**67.** Landscaping ordinances are public laws that regulate landscape design, installation, and general maintenance, and are employed to preserve the visual environment of a community. Post-construction ordinances focus on decreasing land disturbances of individual site plans using methods including, but limited to, preserving trees and controlling stormwater runoff. A post-construction ordinance can be adopted to put landscaping back into a community after existing trees and plants were removed during construction.

*The answer is (D).*

# Solutions

**68.** Leadership in Energy and Environmental Design (LEED®) was developed by Green Building Certification Incoporated (GBCI®) serving as the American organization providing third party certification, criteria and standards for project environmental performance. Buildings become LEED certified by achieving points in six different categories: water efficiency, energy and atmosphere, materials and resources, indoor environmental quality, and innovation and design process. (For more information about LEED or the GBCI go to www.gbci.org.)

The Construction Specification Institute (CSI) is a national association that creates standards and formats to improve construction documents and project delivery. The National Association of Office and Industrial Parks (NAOIP) is a trade association for industrial, commercial, and mixed-use real estate professionals who help promote sustainable project developments. The Urban Land Institute (ULI) is a nonprofit research and education organization that advocates for the responsible and sustainable use of land to help build communities worldwide.

*The answer is (A).*

**69.** Best practices are methods, processes, or techniques that contribute to the most effective or efficient way to accomplish a task. Encouraging tropical coastal regions to grow bamboo is a best practice because bamboo is an available and renewable plant in coastal areas that allows locals to produce a low technology, strong building material without importing non-local materials, which would require high amounts of energy to transport.

All other answer choices are not best practices because they do not clearly connect the task's methods, processes, or techniques with efficient task completion.

*The answer is (A).*

**70.** Sustainable construction practices focus on reducing environmental impacts during a project's construction phase. Examples include using bio-based hydraulic fluids, which are derived from renewable plant resources and are generally more environmentally friendly than petroleum-based fluids; creating a construction waste and debris management plan, which identifies the types of debris a construction project will generate and ways to handle the waste; and utilizing post-consumer aluminum, which requires less energy in the smelting process than virgin aluminum.

Disposing of inert solids and treating wood with CCA (chromate copper arsenate) are not sustainable construction practices. Inert solids (asphalt, brick, dirt, etc.) can be recycled and reused to reduce the demand for virgin resources. Lumber treated with CCA, a chemical wood preservative used to keep wood from rotting, has been classified by the EPA as a restricted use product, and as of December 2003, wood intended for residential use may not be treated with CCA.

*The answer is (B).*

Made in the USA
Las Vegas, NV
17 May 2024